Diary of Mike the Roblox Noob

Murder Mystery 2

Unofficial Roblox Book

Table of Contents

Introduction

Congratulations on downloading *Roblox* and thank you for doing so.

Welcome to the wonderful world of Roblox. As some of you may know, you can create your own world in Roblox and make it what you want it to be. With this book, you are going to step into the world that Mike has created which revolves around him and his adventure as he tries to survive rounds in the Murder Mystery 2 Server.

Mike is very new on the server, and he does not understand the rules that are in this world. He falls prey to the murderer several times before he understands how to survive in the highly aggressive world that he is exposed to. You will see how hard Mike tries to make friends who can help him survive, only to be taken as if he is a murderer.

Join in on Mike's fun adventures as he discovers who he can make friends, find ways of surviving the world of the murderer and the sheriff. This is made possible through the amazing game called Roblox.

If you are going to play Roblox, make sure that you get your parent's permission so that you are not getting harmed. As you have probably already been told, there are all kinds of people on line, and you need to be able to protect yourself and telling your parents about things like strange people talking to you or wanting to meet you is one of the things that you need to do to keep yourself safe.

You can go to www.roblox.com to create an account, and join in the world that is going to take you out of this world and allow you to be someone else even if it is for a little while.

Also, there are all kinds of guides on line that you are going to be able to use to play the game so that you can try to survive in the world of predators, just like the way Mike plays Roblox in this book.

The following chapters are an account of how Mike the Roblox Noob takes a journey through the Murder Mystery 2 Server. It depicts his challenges on how he goes through different aspects of the game, as he tries to survive in the interesting game of discovering the murderer and evading death for the time period that Mike is in the game. Mike also narrates how he creates friendships in the game, how he is betrayed by one of his close friends. The journey on his first day to his last day in this server has many twists and turns that will expose you to Mike's world of adventure. When you are done with this book, you are going to be able to play Roblox in a fun way.

There are plenty of books on this subject on the market, thanks again for choosing this one! Every effort was made to ensure it is full of as much useful information as possible, please enjoy!

Day 1 In Murder Mystery: Learning The Hard Way

Sitting outside the buildings on the park benches was always a treat for me every morning; it was always like a ritual. Most of the people who had just joined the server were hopping around, looking at the screens, trying to read what was being displayed. There was this one guy who had a boom box stereo on his back; he looked hilarious. Watching him was fun as he jumped around the fountain.

With nothing to do that early in the morning, I spent my first day on the server writing my diary entries. Looking at the screens was irresistible. I stood up and went ahead to look at what was written on some of the screens that were being displayed. 'Maybe there are important instructions that everyone needed to know; I don't know,' that was just a thought in my head. A strange voice that came from a loud speaker was always repeating the same statement saying, 'Waiting for your Turn.' As I walked across the open space looking at the screens, one screen had the words

"Elite

What do I get

1.5XP rates

15 coins

Early access to new crates

. . ."

I stopped reading that board because I never understood what all this math meant, it was just gibberish to me. The next board read

"Radio

. . ."

It was a huge Red sign; I could not read what was on the rest of the board because some guys started hopping across the screen. The benches were a safe spot, so I retrieved and sat down, waiting for the repetitive words, 'Waiting for your turn,' to materialize so that I get to see this turn that is highly publicized. As I sat patiently looking around, a few guys appeared from thin air; I guess it was a thing to pop out of thin air on this server.

"Hey man, how you doing?" a voice shouted from the back of the bench where I was sitting.

"I'm cool, can I help you?" I asked. The guy started laughing.

"I doubt you can help; you look new around here. What is your deal bro?" He asked as he approached me.

"It's that obvious huh!" I sighed.

"Yeah, dude. If you were already a veteran, you would be psyched up for the round that is coming, instead of sitting like a lonely mouse on that bench." He said with a friendly tone.

"Oh! Well, I'm a noob then. I will heed your advice then." I rose up and started walking around.

"My name is Sam, by the way. What's yours?" He started.

"I'm Mike," I answered,

In a matter of seconds, we zipped out of the parking place, and I found myself inside a building that looked like an office. I had the label of the word "Innocent," and a countdown started from 8-1. I had no clue what was happening. Some people were hopping around while others were walking fast across the office rooms.

I stood there clueless wondering what the hopping frenzy was about. Before I could even shout Sam, who happened to be walking away, I heard a sharp pain of a stabbing sticking into my back. I fell in pain as I broke into pieces, and I found myself in the parking place, again. I looked at the fountain and paused.

I could not believe what was happening. "What the...! I was so shocked that I paused in the middle of my statement.

I tried to understand what was happening and in my mind, there were a couple of thoughts, but the most dominant thought was "What just happened!!"

I walked around a bit looking at people, and I tried to understand what was going on. 'Waiting for your turn,' the voice started all over again. "Gosh!" was all I could come up with. Life on this server was becoming too harsh for a noob like me. "What to do now, I need to get my wits together," I said to myself. In a matter of seconds, I was zipped to another building and this time, it looked like a building that had lots of rooms. It looked spacious, and the green label "Innocent," appeared again in a few seconds, and it disappeared. I had no idea what it meant, maybe the server had recognized who I was, and people were avoiding me or something, I don't know. I was set to find what it all meant.

The rooms in the building were spacious, with all sorts of furniture; people were busy rushing in and out. The only thing that was on my mind at that time was the stabbing knife that had caught me off guard. "Where did it come from?" I asked myself.

I saw a guy who had a stereo attached to his back walking in the hallway on the opposite side, and I followed him.

"Hey man, I'm a noob here, and I was wondering what is going on, care to help a brother out?" I asked.

The stereo guy ran away from me shouting, "MURDERER!!!" before I could get any closer.

"What the . . . dude!" I remarked. I was even more confused about what was happening than before. Turning to head to the next direction, I saw this guy who had blue hair and a black top; he was heading straight at me. "At least, let me ask this guy," I murmured to myself.

"Hey man. . ." before I could finish the statement, I saw an enormous purple knife pointing at me, and before I could blink, it was already on my chest. The pain I felt lasted a few seconds as I fell into pieces. I found myself back on the park benches,

"OH! Lord, I'm done with this, I call it a day," I said to myself with a very irritated and angry voice.

I went to rest that day thinking about my first day on the server. Things were going too fast, and I needed to think through. As I sat on my bed thinking about what I was going to do, I tried to recollect the memories of the day. All I could remember at most was, Stab! Stab!

Dear Diary,

If you could explain what happened today, you can save me a lot of trouble, but sadly, we are both in the same dilemma. Let us rest over it and plan on getting the answers tomorrow.

Day 2 In Murder Mystery: Creating Allies to Make Alliances for Surviving

Getting used to the park bench and looking at the fountain is a pleasure I think I have to cherish. As I was sitting watching other people, an idea popped in my head, 'hiding.' So, when the usual voice started out, 'Waiting for your turn,' I was ready for my plan of action.

I appeared in a room that had brown walls, a glass table, and chairs around it. Other players were jumping like antelopes all over the place. I was already used to the jumping. There was a glass sliding door which opened up to the back yard. My goal was to find a hiding spot that had a good view of either the corridors or the open spaces, to observe what was going on.

Other players were jumping over the fence, I'm not sure where they wanted to go to, but according to me, it was a lame move. There was no hiding spot in the backyard, so I opted to head inside the house to look for a different hiding place.

"Hello there," a sweet voice stopped my movement. "Where are you headed to? I'm scared, I hope you are not a murderer," she continued. I thought for a moment, "A murderer? Where are you getting this idea from?

Who is a murderer? I keep getting this vibe each time I'm meeting someone." I answered.

"Oh! You are a noob. Well, not to worry, I'm relatively new too, but I somehow know how things go around here," she said.

I finally met someone I could talk to without causing a scene; I felt lucky.

"I have been meaning to meet someone to explain to me what is happening on this server, but no one seems to care, either I'm scaring people away, or I'm getting killed; it's crazy living on this server," I said as I moved closer to her. I got the nerves of introducing myself.

"Hi, I'm Mike, what's your name?" I asked.

"Before I answer, we need to move, fast," she replied. She had red hair, a blue top, and she looked stunningly beautiful, I was in love. But wait, being alive was my top priority.

"Let's go upstairs and hide somewhere, as I tell you what works...."

Before she could finish her sentence, I heard a sharp noise like an arrow landing on a hard surface. Before I turned, the lady I was talking to was on the ground in pieces; the sound of the knife-throw was so loud, anyone could hear it from the hallway. I was so tensed and afraid; I started jumping all over, trying to dodge any knives flying around. My heart was racing, as my palms and neck started to sweat. As I turned the corner, I saw other guys running while screaming, "There is the murderer!!! Murderer!!!" They shouted as I tried running in their direction, but everyone was so fast. I hated being accused of being a murderer while I had no clue on what was going on. My only hope of getting more information about this place was gone in seconds. I ran as fast as I could through corridors until I got lost in the hallways of the building.

I took a breather behind a door, panting like a horse. I was afraid, terrified. Before I could catch my breath, I heard footsteps and people yelling as they jumped around; I tried to peep from the keyhole of the door, but to my shock, stab! Stab! A knife had been thrown to my direction, it passed through the door, "Damn! What in the world. . ." I said as I fell into pieces.

Guess what, dear diary, you guessed right, the park benches. I appeared again on the park benches; I threw my pen to the ground; I was angry. "I can't stay any longer on this server, this is frustrating," I exclaimed to myself. Looking around, I saw the lady I was talking to before she got killed. She was jumping up and down the fountain. I calmed down, composed myself and walked towards her.

"Hey!" I started.

"Hey Noob, sorry about that, the game is that crazy.... how was your first round?" She asked

"It's my third or fourth round; I'm not even sure, it's just crazy, things are going too fast, I'm trying to understand everything that is happening. Would you mind explaining what is happening?" I asked

"Sure, we don't have much time, but when we find ourselves back in the game, I'm going to explain everything, Okay? Oh! And by the way, my name is Jane." she said smiling.

"Okay Jane, as I said earlier, I'm Mike. So, let's start with where we are, what is happening here?" I asked.

"Alright. As I'm told, this is the place where everyone gets to start the game from and choose a map. You see that place that has two swords crossing each other, and it's written 'Vote for the next map here,' that is the place where you decide where the next game is going to be played. The map is the facility we are going to be playing the game. The server usually picks at random the maps in no particular order; you never know where the next game will be. It can be in an office, in a place called Italy, in a mansion that is haunted, there are a couple of maps that are present."

"Yeah, my first map was in an office," I said.

"Yes, that's one of the worst places. It's very congested, and hiding is just hard to all the people present."

"I don't understand. Do you have to fight or hide?" I asked.

"Well, Noob," Jane continued, while smiling, "There are three categories of people in this game,"

"Aha!" I nodded listening carefully.

Before we could talk anymore, I found myself alone with some guy in a room who was dressed in black, from top to bottom. He was jumping on a desk. I saw the count down from 5, 4, 3, 2. . . after it was over, I looked for an escape route to run to. The door in the room was open and my mission this time around was to look for Jane, because I needed further explanation about the secrets of living to the end of the game without getting killed.

I assumed that anyone except Jane was the murderer.

I walked out of the room, into the corridors. "Today, seems like a calm day," I thought. Everyone was just walking around; no one seemed scared of the murderer or whatever name they call him. My objective was to look for Jane. Luckily, within a few seconds, I met her in a corner standing next to a bookshelf in a large corridor.

"Oh My goodness, Mike," she said.

"Finally, I found you. So, how do we go about this?" I asked.

"First of all, who are you?" She asked.

In my head, I wondered, "what does she mean? I'm Mike," then I remembered.

"Oh! I'm an innocent," I said.

"That is the first category of people," she continued.

"Yes, categories. . . got it." I nodded, as I led her to a direction where we could talk. I was scared of just standing in one position.

"We also have a sheriff and a murderer. The murderer is the most feared character on this server," she said looking in every direction for any suspicious movements.

"So, Jane, we should stay away from the murderer?" I asked

"That's the point, Mike, as a matter of fact, maybe you are lying to me that you are an innocent. It's hard to tell who is a murderer you know," she stopped, looking suspiciously at me.

"Jane, seriously, I don't even know how to go about this place, how can I lie to you?" I said.

Before we could go on, we heard a stabbing sound.

"I think it has come from that direction," Jane pointed to the southern part of the hallway.

"We have to run fast. Look at everyone in a frenzy running towards our direction," Jane stated as she held my arm.

"Wait, you see the lady with red hair and purple trousers, that is the sheriff. The sheriff is the only one who can kill the murderer, okay?" Jane continued.

"I get you, Jane, so what do we do?" I asked

"Stay close Mike, don't wander away. We have to stick together," Jane said heading towards the Sheriff, but at the same time being cautious.

"I thought the sheriff is our savior, why are you approaching her in fear?" I whispered.

"You will be shocked to know that the sheriff can kill anyone out of fear that anyone close might be the murderer. You always have to be a more careful noob," she said looking at me.

"Avoid looking at her in the face, she can decide to shoot, and it will be game over for both of you," Jane warned me.

"Oh! There goes another stabbing Jane; it is close to where we are" I said, looking over my shoulders. We left the sheriff alone, and we ran down the hall.

"There is the Murderer Mike," Jane said in fear.

"He is coming towards this direction, look at how people are dropping like flies. Run Jane, run!" I said as we got into a board room kind of place. There were coins all over the room.

"Oh no! The murderer has seen us, and we are in a trap right now. Let's look for a place to hide Mike," Jane said in a tense voice.

"Jane, there is a door on this side of the room, let's head out this way," I held Jane's hand, and we rushed outside the room. Just at the door, we saw the Sheriff, dead.

I was in shock on how the murderer was brutally killing people. "We don't have a sheriff, what is going to happen? How can we kill the murderer?" I asked in a hopeless voice.

"Mike, when the sheriff dies, anyone can pick the gun and still kill the murderer," Jane answered.

"So where is the gun? I can't see it?" I said, looking around for the sheriff's gun.

"Someone has already picked up the gun," Jane answered as she moved around to see if there was anyone around who had the gun.

Dead bodies were all over the place; I was tensed. People were running around everywhere; others seemed clueless. Before we could even move, I saw the murderer, holding a big knife running towards us.

"Jane, the murderer is coming our way, run Jane, run," I said as Jane and I ran in opposite directions. I heard a gunshot, and it was tough to know who had been killed. I ran s fast and stopped to the corner of the hallway. Looking back, I saw the murderer chopping and stabbing anyone who was coming his way. It was gruesome. I hid in the corner, as I watched his movements, I felt lucky when I saw him going towards another direction. The coast was clear in a matter of seconds. As I walked out into the open, I saw something being thrown in my direction, before I could blink. I was dead.

Dear Diary,

Today has been one long day with a lot of drama, I don't know if I can survive that long on this server, but I'm interested in finding a way around it. I have learned a lot in the past two days, and there is more to learn.

Day 3 in Murder Mystery: Trial and error

Today, I will make a step in following the sheriff carefully; the murderer has to go down today. That's the plan diary, and we are going to save the day.

I waited for the next round near the fountain. I stood there motionless, planning in my head what I was going to do. I met Jane in the morning, and she was all over the place; it's like she had taken an adrenaline shot, she could not settle. A part of her was full of fear of the unknown, and the other part was filled with excitement. Anyway, '*waiting for your turn,*' the mysterious voice said. I was ready to get to the end of the game.

"Hey Noob, how are you doing today?" Jane shouted from the back.

"I'm okay, waiting for the game to start, and I have a plan,'" I said in a focused tone.

"By the way, you should know that any time you play the game, you increase your chances of becoming the murderer. That's a point to note Mike.," said Jane.

"Wow! That's an interesting spin," I said.

"So that means you can also be the murderer!" I exclaimed with a sigh.

"Exactly, but don't worry, you can trust me, I will let you know when I get to be the murderer," Jane said, as she laughed.

"Okay, I will also tell you in case I get to be the murderer," I said

As the game started, I became an innocent, and I found myself staring at the bathroom walls. I walked out of the room and into the room corridors. I took a deliberate stand on being observant going onwards, and so, I saw 180 seconds counting down. I guessed that was the time that the game was supposed to last. Other players were walking in and out of rooms, while others jumped all over like kangaroos. There were several rooms in the building which had guns and knives detectors. The presence of the detectors was a blessing, it was the only sure way to notice the presence of the murderer or the Sheriff. The section of the building I walked around was the bank teller area, and it was where I met Jane.

Since I was confident playing this round, I decided to lie to Jane.

"Hi Jane, I am the murderer," I said sarcastically.

"What? Are you serious?" she asked,

"No, I'm joking" I replied

"You are lying. You can't joke about this. You must be the murderer," she said with a tensed voice.

She stepped away from where I was as I laughed.

"We have to stick together. Let's go to another area," I suggested

We went through the metal detectors, and there was no alarm sound, and at that point, I hoped that it was not a dummy. But as we waited there looking at each other, trying to guess who the murderer was, we had a stabbing near the hallway. My adrenaline kicked in, and it was time to look for a hideout. It was hard to see who was stabbed, but the sound of a knife stab was disturbing enough to throw anyone off balance.

The murderer stepped into the room, and everyone who was in it started hiding in every place imaginable. The murderer took advantage of the crowd and started killing people. I saw other innocents dropping to the ground; it was like a massacre. I ran out to the hallway, and when I looked back, Jane was dead, again. Being alone was not a good idea, I hated it. I ran upstairs, to a section with cubicles, it was an office area. Getting into the room, I saw dead bodies around. I quickly jumped over them and started looking for a good hiding spot. Going into the board room, I could hear the annoying stabbing sound. Surviving this round was the only thing that was in my head. As I got to the board room, another lad with a green shirt stormed into the room, panting like a horse. "Where can I hide?" he asked.

"I don't know, I'm also looking for a spot," I answered, trying to get under the table.

We heard stabbing sounds downstairs. With no place to hide in the board room, I tried to rush down stairs and seek an alternative hiding spot, but the murderer was way ahead of my plans; he was just coming up the staircase. I retreated upstairs so fast, and the only space I could think off was a vent that was sealed.

"If only I could get through," a thought crossed my mind. When I heard the footsteps outside the door of the board room, I walked to the vent, and instead of stopping, I found myself inside. That was the best thing that happened. I could not believe it; I was already inside the vent.

As I walked in the vent, I heard screams of a dying innocent, I felt lucky to have survived the murderer's knife just in time. In the vent, there was a vast network of tubes that led to different places; as I passed through one of the exit spots, I noticed a guy in a yellow t-shirt who was holding a gun, "The sheriff," I murmured to myself.

The room where the sheriff was standing was a bank's safe. All I could see was expensive paintings hanged on the wall, loads of cash bags, gold bars, and even fancy attire.

I felt safe when I saw the sheriff. All I could do was just sit and wait, looking at all the cash and expensive items in the safe. The peace of mind and the thought of being at an advantage over the murderer was all that was in my mind; I needed it. It was tempting to steal the items I must say, but it was hard thinking about stealing at this point. All I could think of was surviving the round. Someone else walked into the room; the guy looked tired.

"Is the murderer coming our way?" I asked

"I have not seen him yet," he said,

"Which side are you from?" He asked.

"I'm from the board room on the first floor. Where are you from?" I asked

"I'm from an office room on the third floor," he answered.

As we waited in the room, we decided to poke around the safe shelves, we couldn't help it. After all, the sheriff was on our side. On the contrary, the sheriff decided to leave the room through a vent, the other guy ran after the sheriff, and I was left alone in the safe. I started thinking about the best strategy to use to survive the round, but all I could come up with was following the sheriff.

I decided to follow the sheriff, but while I was in the vent, instead of catching up with the sheriff, I saw the murderer coming towards my direction.

"What the. . .!"

The only image that crossed my mind was that of a dead sheriff. I rushed back to the safe and took another turn to a different ventilation network. The network I got into was a short one, which led to the registry room which was full of drawers and files. I went through the door, down the stair case following the path to an unknown destination. I rushed down so fast, as I knew where I was rushing to.

Running down the stairs only led me to the same room I was from, the bank's safe. This time around, I went through the circular door that guards the safe. It was hard to imagine the person who opened such a large heavy door. After a short while in the safe, I stepped out, went through several doors to escape the murderer the best way I could. I got through to the teller section, and while I was getting through the door of the next room. I saw a sharp blade right on my neck. DEAD. I had just walked right into him, it was annoying.

I zipped, and I found myself in a red lit room with an 8% chance of being a murderer. As an innocent, I was in the quarantine room that looked like a laboratory.

"Noob, I'm the sheriff in town," I heard Jane's voice in the background. She got to the quarantine, and boy, was I happy to have her as the sheriff.

"So, we own this place now, right?" I said with confidence.

"Something like that, but no one else has to know. We don't want to attract the murderer. What we need to do right now, is look for him and smoke him out of his senses," Jane said with zeal.

"You can say that again Jane. So, where do we go? This place is daunting, all these equipment. What is this place used for?" I asked.

"I don't know Mike, let's be on our way," Jane said as we left the quarantine room to look for the best place we could wait for the murderer to show up with his large knife.

We got into a large room filled with chairs, it was weirdly quiet, and before I could turn to react to a movement that was in the purview of my sight. . . Stab! Stab! I was dead. I could hear Jane scream, "how do I shoot?" But I was already dead. I felt so bad. Standing in the waiting bay, I was speechless and sad about missing an opportunity that could have made me win one round. It was disgraceful that we died within the first few seconds of the game. I had no words to describe myself, and the worst part was that Jane had the gun, but she had no clue on how to use it.

For the next couple of days, I am not going to record anything in the diary, I am so annoyed with myself. I am going to observe how everything works on this server and once I have the right information, I will make a run for the best rounds. Today was the closest to winning this game, but we were so dumb to seize the opportunity.

Dear Diary,

I'm so mad at myself, until next time, I need to re-plan my strategy.

Day 9 In Murder Mystery: At Last, The First Real Victory

It has been a few days since I recorded in the diary, and I feel lucky this time round. I have a master plan dear diary; the next few days will be a turning point in my life. Bright and early, I reported to my usual spot near the fountain, waiting for the games to begin. Zip! I was in a dark room. It looked like a cave, or a quarry, I'm not sure. Jane appeared right next to me.

"I'm an innocent Jane, what about yourself?" I asked.

"Hey, Mike, hehe... How are you doing today?" she asked, "I'm okay," I replied.

We got to a room where a long wooden bar was the pathway for climbing up or down to different floors of the building. A couple of guys went up, but we decided to climb down to the lower level.

"We need to have a better plan on how we can win this," I said

"You are right Mike. What do you propose?" I asked.

"We need to survive longer Jane, and this is what I propose. Let's find the sheriff; this should be our first mission, okay. As we execute this, we need to take care of each other throughout the process. Okay?" I continued

"All right Mike, I get you, that's fine," Jane answered.

"Jane, in this round, one of us has to survive until the end of the game. We need to go, is to split, but to have each other's back at the same time, got it?" I asked.

"Got it!" Jane was already jumping around.

"So, no staying in groups, we are going to be spread out while still watching each other's backs," I reiterated.

"Especially in open areas. . ." Jane interjected.

"Good point Jane, you already a pro in Murder Mystery already!" I said with a smile.

"It is impossible to lose with this strategy Mike," Jane said with conviction.

"We have to succeed this time round," I concluded before the game started.

I found myself in the dark corridors of a building, as an innocent.

"Mike, guess what?" Jane asked

"What Jane?!" I answered anxiously.

"I'm the sheriff, Mike," Jane answered.

"Yipee! Where are you, Jane?" I asked. "I can see several blondes in the hallway, where are you?" I continued.

"I'm here Mike, let's go towards that direction," Jane commented as she pointed to an empty hallway.

"Are you sure you are the sheriff?" I asked

"Are you telling me the truth about your innocent state?" Jane shot back.

"Yes, Jane. Let's move before we die like the way we did the other time round." I said as we walked, trying to find a good place to hide. We went down the hallway, met a group of people who were crowded in the entrance of a large room, and since we had agreed to stay away from crowds, we got to a room that had a large circular screen. The large screen had a ring in the middle of the cylinder, the screen was high, close to the roof and it was not easy to spot enough for anyone actually to spot. It was a good hiding place, and that is where we were headed.

"Look, Jane, we can hide up there. Let's climb this boxes and hide in that zone." I said as we rushed to climb to the safe zone we had discovered.

Another player climbed with us to the spot.

"Hey, guys. This is a cool spot," the lad commented

"I know," I watched the new guy from a distance who was rather suspicious to me. As we stayed there longer, he appeared harmless, and we got comfortable around him as time went by.

"I'm Zack," he said.

"I'm Mike, and this is my friend, Jane," I answered.

"No one is going to see us from up here. We have the whole place to ourselves," Zack commented.

"Let's be patient and see what will unfold. Let's sit tight guys." I added as we strolled around the ring.

We saw people strolling, hopping and running around; no one could actually see us. Frankly, we had deviated from our master plan of looking for the sheriff, and we had settled at hiding out.

As we circled the ring to pass the time, I fell to the ground, my heart skipped a beat, I got back up so fast, I never moved again. I waited patiently until the decision for the next move was made.

Since Jane was the sheriff, we decided to go down after we heard the stabbing noises.

"Can you see the murderer?" I asked.

People were running towards our direction, as I hid behind Jane, the sheriff.

"Jane, I can see a red haired lady through the window of the room at that corner," I said, directing Jane to look through the window.

"Might she be the murderer?" I asked.

"Let me go and see if she is the killer," I said, walking towards the blue lit stairs.

Through the window, I saw the red haired lady killing another innocent.

"It is her, she is the murderer!!" I ran back shouting.

Jane who was popular among other players was in front of the crowd with a gun, pointing in the direction where the murderer was coming from.

We all ran away when Jane missed a shot that was meant to kill the murderer, it was not a good sign. The most disturbing thing is that Jane was missing shots and she was pointing the gun in the wrong direction. I understood the fact that she was new in the role, but missing to kill the murderer was a problem to the rest of us, because, by all standards, we needed the murderer dead.

Jane was out of options, and she started running towards our direction when she saw the murderer chasing after her. As we climbed up to get to the upper floor, Jane shocked us by turning around and shooting the murderer right in the head. For once, we won the game, it was unbelievable.

You cannot imagine how happy we were after that round, the sheer excitement, the feeling of achievement, it was unlike anything we had ever experienced. Talk about a good day, even though it was challenging.

Dear Diary,

Today was a good day, we achieved something that was out of our reach. I think it's a start of a new dawn and dominating the game won't be a problem going forward. Yipee!! Celebrating is not a bad thing, right!

Day 10 in Murder Mystery: The Betrayal

When we got to the fountain in the morning, I was so happy to meet Jane.

"You turned the game around Jane, what a fantastic show of marksmanship. It was a dead shot that gave us a victory. How do you feel after that?" I asked.

"You have no idea Mike, I'm over the moon. A victory at last. We should look for another way that we can get a better result. We need to see if you can also become a sheriff at some point. "Jane said modestly.

We roamed around the fountain, waiting for the next round as we planned for a new mission.

Looking back at the statistics of the game, we had survived being alive in the game for 161 seconds out of 180, that was a record timing. Today, we wanted to have a better chance of surviving than the previous day. As we waited for the game to start, we shared stories on the events that happened before the victory. Jane, who has a friendly spirit around her, was thronged by other people who were congratulating her for the win in the game.

I sat there, rather happy for her as I coined a better way of surviving. Being a noob, and particularly a shy one, I was already fond of Jane. It was hard trusting other people, but with Jane, things have been going on well in the game. I walked around, waiting for Jane to be free as I thought about other strategies that we could do together.

"I'm astonished that the murderer did not get the hint that you were onto her while you were shooting in other directions," someone said, making the whole crowd that was around Jane to burst out into laughter.

"Either, that was one of the worst murderers I have ever seen, or you are one of the worst sheriffs, it's one of those two" he continued laughing.

"No Sam, I'm one of the best shooters ever," Jane said while laughing, as he shoved Sam out of the way.

"See you all in the game guys," Jane said as she rushed towards my direction.

"You ready to have a shot at the next game?" Jane asked.

"Well, I'm still thinking of other ways to win even better," I answered.

And the round began.

"I am an innocent Jane, What about you?" I shouted.

Jane was quiet for a few minutes.

"I am on the other side of the cave, where are you?" Jane asked.

"I was trying to go through some opening, but I tripped, anyway I will have to go through the door. This place looks like a train tunnel, and people are everywhere." I noted

"I think I have seen you, Jane, is that you over... oh no, no, that's not you," I remarked.

"I just saw the red haired girl again," I said to myself.

"Oh! Jane, Jane......there you are." I said as I walked briskly towards her.

Jane started out," Mike; this is not a safe place, let me take you to a place that is quiet and more secure. This place is very dark, and we need a better place to hide."

"Okay Jane, right after you, lead the way," I answered as I ran towards her direction.

We got into a place that had boxes, some dynamite and a tall cubic ladder that led people to the other floors. Jane was acting weird, and I could tell, but I brushed it off.

"This looks like a safe spot," I said.

We climbed two floors up, and other people followed us. We got to a small room that was confined. In a matter of minutes, the room was full of about ten people, who were jumping around. Before anyone could go down, a sheriff appeared, and people felt secure that he was with around. I also felt safe in the numbers and the presence of the sheriff in the room.

I watched Jane walking behind the sheriff, and to my shock, she pulled out a knife and stabbed the sheriff. I was startled, I could not move. Jane went on a rampage of killing people. I ran so fast, and before I could get to the ladder, she was on my back with a dagger right behind my back, and I was dead.

I felt a lot of pain as I died, wondering why Jane had brutally murdered me. It was shocking; I appeared on the fountain spot. I was silent and reflective this time round. Everyone I had tried reaching out to had somehow turned their backs on me. I never wanted to see Jane again. I felt so betrayed and bitter. Within a short time, Jane appeared, I guess she was shot by an innocent who had picked up the dead sheriff's gun. I walked into my room without looking at Jane, all I wanted to do is sit down and records the day's ordeal in my diary. A tear dropped off my cheeks, and I vowed, never to be taken advantage of again. I was fed up with treating people well, while they were taking my kindness for weakness. No level of sorry would make me forgive her, for what she had done.

Day 11 In Murder Mystery: Face to Face With The Murderer

Back at the fountain, I plotted a new way of getting the best out of every situation; I was ready to get into the game; stealth was my number one option. I stood quietly in a corner as I waited for the games to start. The map was loading, and I crossed my fingers, hoping to be either a murderer or the sheriff. When the time came, I was an innocent, I felt unlucky. This time around, I was going solo, I had figured out an idea of how to beat the system that was always crushing me each time. I also learned that betrayal is real and I did not want to trust anyone again.

When the game started, I moved around slowly, looking for either the murderer or the sheriff. My target was to be in places where very few people were located. I was an innocent in this round. When the game started, I was in an open room full of seats that were close to the wall. My immediate response was to rush fast out of the room. I went straight to the hallways and peeked to see if there was any activity in the room I had just left. Everyone was running around trying to find an exit.

"Hey man," Zack shouted.

"Hey Zack, I'm kind of in a rush," I replied running past him like a torpedo.

"Oh! Okay," he answered as he looked over his shoulder as I zoomed past him.

I scouted different rooms trying to look for the sheriff or the murderer. As I walked into the rooms, I decided to keep collecting the coins that were all over the place. I had no idea what they were going to be used for, but I felt obliged to pick them.

As I was walking around, I heard a gunshot; that was my cue. "Where did it come from?" I asked myself. I tried to rush to see if I could spot the sheriff, but it was too late. The only thing I found in the room was coins; it was not all that bad.

The sound of a stab came from the room across the hallway, and I was all ears like a wild jackal. Everyone was asking where it came from, and it was confusing because the walls were echoing the sound, it was hard to trace the sound's source. I was in a panic mode, I tried hiding behind the chair, but it was too small. The desk in the office was not a place to debate upon; there was no place to hide here.

"Twaaaf!!!" the sound of the gun made me even more confused. I could not tell which direction I needed to go. Standing in the middle of the room, I was immobile for a while, just looking over my shoulders, trying to see if the sheriff or the murderer could appear from any given direction. In a few seconds, I saw someone getting stuck on the wall by a huge knife that had been thrown at him. I turned to the other side and ran for my life. I hid behind the door because I had one objective, to track either the murderer or the sheriff in stealth mode.

The murderer passed by the doorway and I held my breath for a moment. The large knife passed by my eyes in slow motion, as he looked for the next victim. He rushed around the corner and into the other part of the hallway. I followed him gracefully, shadowing his movements. I was keeping a low profile. All I could see was the effect he had on the innocents; everyone who was on his way was terrified. Some people tried to go through walls when they didn't see a clear hiding space, others would pray for the ground to open up for them to escape, but all they could do was wait for the knife of death to cut short their lives.

My ninja skills were working out just fine. I never jumped, never called out on anyone, nor did I make any sound to attract the murderer's attention. I observed him, and that was my game plan. We got to a position where the murderer had the sheriff in a tight corner. Within seconds, the sheriff was dead and all those who were with him in the office corner. The murderer left that room scratch free. The room was silent. The hallways were quiet, and everyone was either dead or hiding in the vents, it was a scary moment.

I peeked, waiting to see if the murderer was going to make any movement, but he just stood there guarding the gun against anyone who wanted to collect it. It was annoying. "Wait!" I thought, "maybe there is a vent that leads to the room." I decided to look for vents in the room where I was hiding. I walked in the network, trying to see if I could find my way to the room that had the sheriff's gun. Well, I think it was a bad idea because it led me to a different room. Getting back to my spot, I had lost sight of the murderer; when I rushed into the room, the gun was gone. I was shocked; I was at a loss, no gun, no idea where the murderer was, and I was going to run around like a headless chicken. When I turned around to step out of the door, I could only see the murderer standing at the front door. I couldn't even catch my breath; I was stunned. I tried hopping around different areas trying to escape, but he just watched me. When I took my last step on the floor, a knife was thrown, and it landed on my chest, dead once again mate.

Dear Diary,

I have seen better days, but not a head to head match with the murderer, that was not even a full fight. I wish I had a gun at that point. I retired to bed that day still mesmerized by the sheer accuracy of the murderer. "Maybe I should change tactics," I thought. Planning tricks for the Innocent role was an objective I had decided to master for the next few days. I'm not going out in the 'wild' as of now; I will be going to a stealth operation camp, and learn how to be the best INNOCENT the server has ever seen. That's my mission for the next few days, until next time dear diary, time for the planning to begin.

Day 12 In Murder Mystery: Using Tricks To Kill The Murderer

The loaded map was the same as the last time. I quickly ran as an innocent to scout around the area. My objective was to have a soldier's heart. Armed with a knife and a gun that was not loaded, I knew I wanted to spot the sheriff; boy did I have a plan for him. After getting the best hiding spot, I headed back, trying to locate a place that was crowded.

Everyone was everywhere; there were many rooms in the building, but they were all crowded. As we walked through the corridor, I shouted "MURDERER!" and I caused panic to everyone. I was trying to spot the sheriff through the chaos. It was hard to see anyone with a gun, but at last, the sheriff appeared guns blazing towards my direction. I hid in some brown boxes as he took charge of the situation, trying to spot the murderer.

My plan was going on well because I wanted the sheriff to shoot someone out of panic. If an innocent die, the sheriff would also die, that was my goal. If the sheriff dies, I will be going to collect the gun and kill the murderer. Talk about doing anything to win the game. Was I becoming evil, dear diary? Or is it just part of the game. Well, I think I'm fair, and it's not my position to shoot the innocent, I'm just trying to scare the sheriff into making my wishes, as I make way for an interesting day ahead. My plan was halfway done, the sad part is that the sheriff missed shooting an innocent, even though he had panicked and shot in the air. Damn! It hurt just a little bit, but I was hopeful that the plan was going to work." Who misses shooting in a crowd of people?" I was perplexed.

Anywhere the sheriff went, I was on the tail. My work was to get the sheriff's gun. Every time I saw a crowd, I shouted MURDERERRRR!! and each time that happened, the sheriff shot in the air. I'm not sure if it was a sign that he was pooping in his pants, or it was just a wild shot that was meant to scare away the murderer.

Out of nowhere, the sheriff was dead; the murderer took advantage of my plan quietly. All along, he was following the crowd, waiting for my signal to spot the sheriff. Talk about a master plan being hacked. Well, we all went in different directions.

"What the hell is happening Mike," Jane asked.

I never wanted to see her; I rushed passed her like a bullet train. She was left mouth agape.

I went for the corner and sneaked back, all I could see was the murderer on a killing spree, he decapitated everyone who was near him.

"Where is the gun?" that is all I could think off. Braveheart was my middle name at this point. I circled the place and appeared in the part where the sheriff was killed, but there was no gun in the vicinity,

"I guess there were still a couple of us left and someone had picked up the gun," I said to myself.

I was the master of sneaking around. I followed the murderer since I had spotted his dressing attire and how he looked like. Stealth mode was my way of playing. At this point, I had noted who was in possession of the gun, and I was on the lookout. The murderer who had also spotted the guy with the gun, hid in a corner, waiting for the clueless lad to step out of the room to meet his death. It happened so fast that the murderer threw a knife through the door. Nice! It's just about time; I saw the gun floating around, and I was patiently waiting for the murderer to change route and head for the other innocents who were on the top floor.

As the murderer stepped out of the room, he looked around, and he heard the footsteps of some people who were moving around like insects on the top floor. He pulled out his knife and headed upstairs. My opportunity was coming to life, as I sneaked around, I finally got the gun. I felt as if the world was in my hands and the lives of the other people depended on it. I rushed so fast up stairs, trying to practice my aim. This was the first time I was holding a gun, but I had to make it count.

Up the stairs, I could hear screams, and I heard the sound of the first stab. I saw the back of the murderer who was standing in the door way. I pointed the gun, and I think he heard the click of my gun, as soon as he turned, I shot the first shot and I missed. Damn! Before the next shot loaded, there was a delay which I did not know about. The murderer started running towards me and throwing knives at me. I hopped as many times as I could, dodging the bullets.

Finally, the gun loaded, as he got closer to where I was, I shot straight at him as he released a knife straight to my direction. My shot was on target, and sadly, his knife was also right on target, we both died.

This was the best time of my life on this server. I had achieved something I had never achieved before, even though I succumbed to his vicious knife. Killing a murderer in my first handling of a gun was an achievement that I had longed for, ever since I set foot on the server. Sitting down on my bed that night, all I could think of was that nothing is impossible, no matter how many times I had failed.

Dear Diary,

Today, we have achieved more than we expected with the difficulties of the day. It is important to spot opportunities and take them. Next time, I am going to be better. I'm excited about the next day, and it's going to be fun. I think, by now, I have a better chance of becoming the sheriff. Since my chance of being a sheriff is high, I'm going to practice more on my aim before I sleep.

Day 13 In Murder Mystery: Saved In The Nick Of Time

Yipee!!! Sheriff mode was my mode of the game. Finally, the time had come for me to be in charge of the place. I never wanted that position to get to my head because attracting the murderer is easier. I calmed myself down and started running around, getting familiar with the place as I avoided the crowd.

"Mike!" I heard a voice from the back. I turned and saw it was Jane. I sighed, asking myself what she wanted this time round. I stopped and waited for her.

"I'm sorry Mike for messing things up. I was carried away by the situation. I'm sorry Mike," she said in a low tone.

I looked at her, told her we would talk another time, and I started walking away. I never wanted to be distracted.

"Do you have a plan Mike on the next round?" She asked in a polite tone. "Not really, but I want to do something I have been thinking about.

"Can I tag along?" she asked.

"If you can keep up, be my guest," I answered.

"Thanks, right after you," she said.

We raced down the corridors carefully watching if we could spot the murderer.

We passed through a cafeteria and stopped. I felt thirsty; we got in the cafeteria.

"Do you want a milkshake?" I asked.

"Sure, I could do with a shake," she answered.

We got a few shakes, and we were on our way.

Out on the corridors, everyone was busy walking into different rooms. We walked past the book shelves, turned into a corner and rushed down the hallway, trying to look for a place we can hide.

After I got into the room, I closed the door.

"What are you doing Mike, we need to at least look for the sheriff like we always do. At least we will have a chance that way. Do you have something else in mind?" she asked.

I pulled out the gun.

"I'm the sheriff, Jane," I said

She was shocked but smiled as she started hopping around like a Bambi.

"Okay okay, settle down, we need to be objective this time round." I said, "let's find a different place, but I have a plan on how we can kill the murderer," I continued.

Jane settled down, and she pulled me behind the boxes in the corner.

I wondered what we were going to do in the corner.

"We need a safe place where we can't be seen, to plan better," she said.

"Oh! Okay" I said, I had different thoughts at that time.

"So, my plan is a bit evil, but it can work well. When we get to a place that is a bit congested, we have to shout SHERRIIIFFF!" I said.

"Wow! Why should we do that, Mike?" Jane asked.

"We need to scare the murderer into exposing the knife." I continued

"Well, what if the murderer waits and does not do anything, what happens?" Jane countered.

"I think the point is to have someone killed; I highly doubt the murderer will miss out the opportunity of killing people who are in one place seeking the safety of the Sheriff," I answered.

"That's a good point, I hope it works," Jane stated.

"Let's get to it then," I said.

We went into the corridor and started to look for a crowd of people to execute our plan.

Things went according to plan, and by the time we were getting to the end of the hallway, we found people standing there for no reason. I had no idea what people were doing. Were they looking at a wall painting or the plant at the corner, I'm not sure, they all looked as if there was no murderer around. We waited to see if more people could get to the corner. Jane could not help any longer.

"There is the Sheriff." she shouted.

Everyone stopped what they were doing, and they started looking at the direction she was pointing. A stranger who was being pointed to was clueless, and people began gathering around her. We stood separately from the crowd, to see if the murderer could take the trap. I had already planned our exit strategy through the room that was just opposite, from where we stood.

The plan was falling apart as people had started figuring out that it was a lie. People started walking away, and our plan was just going down the drain.

"We have to think about another plan Jane, this is not working," I said.

From nowhere, I saw a knife passing over my shoulder and into another innocent. The murderer ran so fast into the crowd and started stabbing everyone he could lay his hands on. It was happening so quickly I could not believe it.

"Let's go hide Mike," Jane said in a fearful voice.

"No, we need to take him out. I have the gun, remember?!" I answered.

"Do you have a clear shot, Mike? The murderer is coming our way" Jane said in a fearful voice as she held my shoulders. Jane was afraid; I could feel her trembling right next to me. I was also not composed, I tried to aim with a sober mind, but it was hard.

I pointed towards the murderer as I moved backward. I took one shot, but it missed the murderer by a whisker.

He turned towards my direction and started running after us. The first knife was thrown towards our direction, and we dodged it as we waited for the gun to reload.

"Oh, Lord! Are we going to make it?" Jane asked as she peaked, trying to see if the murder was in view.

"He is coming fast Mike, let's run away, is the gun loaded yet?" Jane asked

Before we could get to the room that was a few meters away, the murderer was already in our view.

"Mike!! watch out!" Jane screamed as the knife flew to our direction towards me. Before it was game over for me, Jane jumped on the way, and she got hit. I could not believe it. Jane was dead. I hid fast in the room, closed the door and waited for the murderer to get in.

I stood across the room, pointing the gun straight at the door. I was shaking like a leaf. My hands were all over the gun, all I could think of was squeezing the trigger in case the door knob was moved.

There was no movement for a few seconds. I wondered where the murderer was hiding; I moved to a different side just in case he opened the door and shot a couple of knives to my direction. The door opened, and I shot straight when I saw a body walk in. A knife just passed by me and stuck to the wall off the room; he had missed. I WON.

Finally, I won, I appeared immediately at the fountain area excited like a kid who had been bought a unicorn as a birthday present. I could not imagine, the excitement that was flowing through my veins could not be calmed down. I started looking for Jane. Jane was by the fountain with a couple of friends. I walked straight to her, and she came by at me.

"How did it go, Mike?" she asked

"You the best, you know that?" I said

She flicked her hair just like a southern sun girl bouncing in the open fields. I hugged her and forgave her for how she betrayed me the other time. We stepped aside and started talking about how we had taken that round. I narrated how the final seconds of the game went with complete excitement. I think I had gotten to her level of excitement. My hands were all over, simulating how I was shaking as I held the gun waiting for the murderer to step into the room. She could tell how happy I was as we walked around the fountain.

What a day, dear diary. We finally did it, it was never easy, but we managed to take down the most feared villain in the server, the murderer. Time to tuck in the bed, wait for tomorrow and see what it presents.

Day 14 In Murder Mystery: The Set Up

Today seems like a good day. I was bright and early than most people. Near the fountain, a couple of guys were waiting for the upcoming turn. I met Zack who was reading one of the sign boards written 'Server Status: New Updated.'

"Hey man, where are the rest of the guys?" I asked

"Hey Mike, how are you doing? Who are you talking about?" Zack asked while walking to the next sign board.

"For starters, there is that guy who had a boom box stereo on his back, where did he go?" I asked.

"That guy? You never heard what happened to him?" Zack turned his attention towards me.

"What?" I asked curiously.

"Well, he was taken to prison. I heard that he was trying to steal from the bank and the worst part was that, when he became the sheriff, he killed so many innocents; he was caught and taken to Prison. What is happening on this server is messed up, but that's just one extreme case dude," said Zack.

"Oh! That does not sound good." I answered.

"Mike, how are you doing today?" Jane shouted from a distance.

"I'm okay, can't wait to get started, Jane. What about yourself?" I asked as I thanked Zack for the information.

"I'm okay Mike, So, what are we going to do today?" I asked.

"Today, I think we are going to play it randomly. Let's wait and see the place we will be heading and the roles we will have. After that, we will customize our strategy as we go on. How does that sound." I asked smiling at Jane.

"You seem confident Noob," she answered laughing.

"I'm I still a noob? Jane, are you serious! Stop playing with a pro. Matter of fact let's go wild in the next round and see who is the noob," I challenged Jane.

"Right on. Challenge accepted noob," she responded as she laughed.

We laughed and walked around as we waited for the next turn. My label turned to, wait for it, INNOCENT. "You can't be serious, I can't become a murderer, for once?" I asked myself with a sigh.

As I appeared in the dungeons of an unknown place, someone just passed next to me who was dressed exactly as I was dressed. He looked just like me. His height, his hair color, his skin tone, I was stunned for a second. To make it more vivid, the guy had maroon hair, a blue shirt that was written 'I love cats' and black pants, just like me. "What the. . ." I turned almost twice. "Where did that guy come from?" I continued asking myself that question.

"Mike, what are you staring at, standing there like a zombie?" Jane came to the place where I was, in a happy mood.

I brushed the thought away and said, "It's nothing, Jane. So, shock me, you are here to kill me?" I asked as I walked straight towards her.

"Hahaha! You are funny, I wish I was the murderer. I will be honest, I'm just as innocent. How about you?" She asked

"Well, I'm not a murderer or a sheriff, I'm bored to death, so it's back to chasing smoking mirrors in the corridors of this dark place. Where are we, it looks dark in here. Let's find somewhere interesting," I said.

We walked out of place, carefully looking out for each other's backs.

We heard knife stabs going around a few meters from where we stood. A lady came towards our direction.

"How did you. . ." she turned without completing the sentence and ran so fast in another direction.

"What just happened?" Jane asked

"I don't know Jane, but we are about to find out," I answered as we tip toed slowly towards the area where the murderer was located. The hallways were clear; we could not find anyone along the way. It was quiet; no screams no sounds. As we got to the room where the stabbing sounds were coming from, we saw dead bodies scattered on the floor. Everyone was dead on the floor, even the sheriff. But we could not see the gun. We guessed there must have been someone who got to the room before us.

"This seems odd, unlike anything we have ever seen," Jane commented.

"You are right on that Jane. What has happened here?" I asked a rhetoric question.

As we got to another tunnel, we found a few guys who were in a room trying to hide. When they saw us, they started screaming. The confusion in my head got me thinking. Everyone started jumping around trying to escape, Jane has shoved aside, and someone started shooting at us. We split up with Jane as she ran with the other guys towards one direction as I ran for cover to the other direction. What was happening was daunting, I found myself alone in another room, thinking about what was going on. As time went by, the thought that was in my head was that I should get cover in a safe place, and hide until the round was over, because everything was strange from the moment the round started. Another stabbing sound came from an area close to where I was hiding. I froze for a minute, and by the time I was going to open the door right next to where I was, I could not believe what I saw.

The guy who was dressed like me was standing in the doorway. On the other hand, he held a very impressive knife, one that I have never seen before. It was big, I can't tell the material that was used to make the knife; he smiled the whole time as he looked at me.

"Hi twin, time to die Noob," He said in a deep voice.

"I shoved him from the door and ran as fast as I could, I hopped, from one corner to the next, trying to dodge the murderer's knives if he decided to throw them. I don't know how he did it, but once I got to the corner, he threw only one knife, spot on to my back and that was the end of me.

That was the weirdest round I had ever experienced. I was confused. When I appeared on the other end, I met guys who were looking at me strangely. I couldn't spot Jane, I tried to reach out to Zack, but the cold treatment I got from different people was shocking. All of a sudden some police men approached me. I could not understand what was happening.

"Are you Mr. Mike?" they asked

"Yes, that's my name, what is this about?" I asked

"You have been charged with unruly behavior on the server. You have violated several laws that govern the life amongst the innocent, and you are under arrest," the policeman said.

"Wait, wait, wait. . ." I said as I stepped back.

"There has to be a misunderstanding. I have not done anything wrong, and you need to check again, sir!" I said in a shaking voice.

"Guards, apprehend him," the lead policeman said to one of his guards.

"No no..." I cried," Jane, tell them I'm innocent." I tried reaching out to Jane.

"Mr. Policeman, I think you are mistaken, my friend here has not done anything wrong, where is the evidence that shows that he has made a grave mistake?" Jane interrupted.

"Step back, young lady," one guard said as she was whisked off her feet. "You better stay put, or you will be arrested for obstruction," the guard said.

"We are going to get to the bottom of this Mike," said Jane as I got cuffed.

"I will come and find you, let me see what I can do on my end," she said.

"This is unfair," I cried to the guards.

I watched Jane and the crowd staring at me in helplessly. I was taken to the police station where I was placed in an interrogation room. I sat helplessly in the room as I waited for someone to explain to me as to why I was being charged and sentenced to prison. The most interesting thing was that no one treated me harshly and no one stepped into the room. I had my diary with me the whole time, and I could only open it to read how life on the only server that I had experienced life in was. I looked back and could only appreciate how many people I had interacted with, throughout the whole experience.

Just as I was day dreaming about the experience I had and the people I met, a tall bright and seriously faced policeman walked into the room with a huge file. I looked at him as though I had seen a monster who was about to send me to hell. I started trembling but composed myself in a matter of minutes.

The tall guy was dressed in a black uniform that resembled that of a prison facility.

"Hello son," He greeted me in a soft tone, that was not what I expected.

"I'm fine," I answered as I tried to be careful of any utterances that I came up with.

He opened his file and started asking me a few questions. The thing is, I was not able to answer any questions according to his theories because I had no clue what he was asking. For instance, he asked me a question regarding how I was able to get the 'corrupt knife' that I used to kill people with. I had no idea what a corrupt knife was, and the interrogation was pointless to some extent as I could not give any information.

"You caught the wrong guy," I kept saying. But they never wanted to hear anything of the kind.

"Do you know what is going to happen to you sir?" the officer asked

"Before we get there, have you considered that you might have caught the wrong person?" I asked with fear. The thought of jail was making my nerves to burst.

"Here is what is going to happen, young man," He started out

"The offense you have committed is very grave, and since you are not cooperating, you are going to be detained and taken to Prison Life server where you will live, for the rest of your life. I have not seen anyone who is interested in seeing you here in the police station, and we are going to keep it that way unless you tell us where you got that knife from." He concluded.

I could not believe the officer; he was still sticking to his side of the story. My mind started drifting to prison life, and I could only have a faint picture of how life was going to be like. In all my honesty, I was innocent, but I realized there was nothing that was going to change the decision. It was already a done deal, I yielded and opened my life to fate.

I kept quiet for a while as the officer started drafting a letter on the spot. "You are going to be transferred today to the Prison Life server, and this case is going to be filed as closed. I hope that I will not see you again and you are going to have a glorious time in jail. We are going to take your belongings and keep them safe." He said.

I lowered my head in disappointed and said, "Can I at least have my diary, it's the only comfort I have."

"Sure, why not, if it makes you happy," the officer concluded as he opened up the door to leave.

I was left in the seat disappointed and in a very bad mood. My life had changed for the worst, it was not interesting anymore, and I knew my life was over. "Prison Life. What is this!" I exclaimed to myself as I watched officers pacing around their desks through the open door.

After a few minutes, some police officer came to the interrogation room, unlocked my chains and walked me out. "You are going to be transported to the Prison Life server in the next few minutes," one officer said. I was escorted to a black van that had no windows. My time in the free world was over, and I was open to new beginnings, I had no idea what was going to happen to me.

Dear Diary,

Today marks the start of a new life on another server. It's hard to tell if one can survive in Prison Life for a long time or not, but we are going to find out. There is nothing that can be done to change this situation, but we are going to make things happen, one way or the other. I'm scared of everything that is going on, but we are going to take. . .

"What are you doing!" one officer who was seated right next to me asked.

"I was allowed to use my diary in Prison life; I write my experiences here, just a fun thing I do for myself," I answered

"Okay, carry on," he said as he looked away.

. . a day at a time throughout the experience.

Made in the USA
San Bernardino, CA
09 October 2017